T0354674

Journey

JOURNEY

SHREESHANKAR

PARTRIDGE
A Penguin Random House Company

ISBN: Hardcover   978-1-4828-5892-1
                Softcover   978-1-4828-5891-4
                eBook   978-1-4828-5890-7

Print information available on the last page.

To order additional copies of this book, contact
Partridge India
000 800 10062 62
orders.india@partridgepublishing.com

www.partridgepublishing.com/india

To

My Guru and

My Loving Family

Author's Preface

It has been sometime since I wrote verses. There has been a long break of more than 20 years and I have tried to spin the wheel as much. I have always felt that real freedom is in expression and speech. When you have that you have everything else. Expression of grief and hurt is the start of the healing process, which in case might take years.

I have always had good critics in my family who have patiently digested my failures and enjoyed my successes. They were insisting that I was not so bad.

At last I have bitten the bullet and published this volume in which I have tried to build on some real life events and arrive at something readable for you. Enjoy reading.

I was growing plants and trees for more than a year at home and a baobab tree which I had planted was really a dear. She was alive and growing and she died all of a sudden. I loved seeing all those trees grow and now most of them are in their prime and will continue to grow except the loved baobab.

The governments and leaders bring in good legislations and ultimately the managers and the middle men are left with overseeing the implementation which does not work in many cases. Corporate or managerial abuse of the employees at the lower level has increased over the years and goes very much unnoticed. This is due to the circumstances which are planned over a period of time and also the lack of knowledge in the case of employees. Any employee who is denied his work permit or where it is with held by the company has no identity to even go to the police station. The rights still exist for the person to approach the respective embassies or the human rights commission which very rarely the uneducated laborer is aware of. I have tried to document what I have noticed in the middle east.

The pain that one goes through when there is nowhere to go is immense. I have tried to live a refugee's life in the heart of my hearts.

Shreeshankar

LOVE AND GREEN

1

BIRTH

From where I was born, which I came,
No knowledge gained whatsoever,
Separated from a mother too loving,
Here I lay erect, a stump with leaves coarse,
Small but hearty and feeling mighty,
In environs so steeped in beauty,
Heaps of manure and smelling dung,
Neighbors so many but so small,
Their caste and creed not defined,
Though definitions great in number,
In this home they nurture little ones,
Who do not know each other,
The softest wind loves and hugs me,
I break into laughter when they tickle,
Warm hands extended from Heavens,
Their absence signaling a dark night,
That happy patter excites me,
Tiny brown feet dipped in mud,
Angels around me concerned,
Neither sprouts nor leaves green,
Expectant for blossoms faraway,
Soft fingers dip into my soul,
To take birth anew with li'l sprouts.
What was that feeling inside me,
What am I to feel anything,
But the Universal and Eternally present Love.

2

SALE

Still early to wake up with the black cloak,
Slowly fading away to the west,
Our heads bowed do we welcome,
The warrior revered with numerous arms,
Peeking above the horizon with crimson eyes,
The darkness dispelled with those radiant arms,
And touched, I shake away my slumber,
All my world swaying in unison,
To the rhythm of a sweet morning,
To welcome one more glorious day,
Leaves above showering down,
Gusts of wind sweeping the earth,
Little winged ones glide down to peck,
In search of their food within me,
It's a guess what is in me to feed others,
I shake and shiver to feel but,
Still not fully aware of everything,
That has to grow in me to be large,
Spanning a large portion of the space,
Between the earth and clouds,
All toddlers of the supreme,
Waiting for the knights in armor,
In a packet among the multitude,
My worth a nought now,
Sold to a stranger anon,
Who came dark as clouds in the day,
Asking to buy a free spirit rooted
Nowhere.

3
JOURNEY

And he took me in his hands affected,
Loving, held me aloft, and quipped,
"There you are my little one",
Then he took me, I don't know where
On a machine with two wheels,
He rode slow with me dangling,
Dancing with every bump and rut,
There was a creak and a tweak,
With every movement of his body,
Was it a never ending well worn path,
Traversed by so few before me,
Stretches further and farther,
Do I wish for this end to begin,
For whom and when in time,
Where within and without for me,
Imprisoned in a packet in a bag,
Gentle breeze wraps me into the bag,
Every moment striking deeper,
A un assumed fear of that unknown,
That never has a beginning,
Do I start that to have a life,
Which never existed to bloom,
Before this day as always,
Waiting for the midas touches,
Which is never very often but,
Only in thoughts deep inside,
To sprout forth on occasions very few,
Like this day when I think clear ahead,
To reach a new somewhere.

4
NEW ABODE

Have I reached a new abode,
Bare but for a few children of my stream,
Waving their little branches,
In that little note of welcome,
A familiar sound of the leaves rustling,
Fresh earth dug up in mounds,
Is it for me to rest here to bloom,
For years to come, I wish I was,
Am I stuck too much to the past,
Which never existed for me,
At last I am down in there in the pit,
Earth showered on my roots,
Sensational showers of water streaking
through my tender feet
I am here to survive and live till I leave,
He is soft, touching tender, talking love,
Do I feel love all around, everywhere,
Through the touch and looks,
Is it twilight that sets things in motion,
The rays of that grand artist,
Pouring colours vivid and wide,
Setting the stage for one more night,
In an abode so new.

5

DAY

Someone knocking on my few leaves,
Beset with life asking me,
Are you alive to live and flourish,
Am here to stay my Lord,
Where from he comes with the wand of light,
Patronizing even the smallest one among us,
Looking down on me from the Heavens,
Mother earth has me in her bosom,
He has me in his heart for love,
Which melts all my innards to feed,
Was he up there afore I came,
Was he the brightest one there,
Do I care for what he gives me.
That ruddy glow faraway striking
A lively chill up my nerves,
They have arrived with cackles,
The feathered without flight,
Running circles around me,
The occasional pluck at my sprouts,
An irritation without reason,
Maybe for this day I think,
But for future to live with,
And here he comes with my life,
The earth softens sagging,
Did I need all that water,
After the dry warm night,
I shake off that slumber,
Did I sleep though,
What's day and night for me,

The warmth of the light adds energy to,
The life juice traversing up my veins,
I declare myself live to the world,
All day long I watch the crows,
Cow at the gates awaiting her food,
Slinking sheep munching at our leaves,
Visitors many to love and brave against,
Dogs slurping away at water in store,
Sparrows taking a skinny dip,
The visitors cooling themselves,
Chatter on the roads,
Cuckoos cooing away happily,
Announcing a new growth on a barren land,
Contented chirps of the birds,
The wilting buds on trees,
Drooping leaves for the night,
Fading light melting to a night,
Does the day end,
The start and the end defined,
For the regular world.

6
DOGS

I am awake awaiting someone,
In his glory to shine down on me,
He comes in his own time to troll
All day long in the bright ocean of a sky,
With aimless clouds drifting to,
Wherefrom they say the day starts,
Moments water streams down my roots,
When he fondles my tender branches,
Dust cleared away with the spray,
I sway to the rhythm of the winds,
Whence the quadruped dashes in,
Squeezing between his legs,
New ways to show the love for him,
Whining sweet to mark his presence,
He is of an higher order of being,
Wonder which was that to,
Whither running circles around me,
Sniffing the air for the scent of,
His master who is not to be seen,
Who it is that defined him as what,
Who defined me as what I am,
What is that form which is in front,
In the rear and everywhere,
I grounded to watch him move,
The dog who can think whilst,
I cannot that's what I hear,
I feel everything around me,
The winds, rain, cold, torrid heat,
The heat does burn my sap and inside,

Drying my innards but not the will,
He seeks my shade in the heat,
Hunkering down beneath my leaves,
I see him daily appearing in morning,
Disappearing in the day to roam,
Presenting a form filthy for food,
Barking away crazily at anyone,
In territory he claimed as home,
Was loved by everyone at home.

7

MONGREL

They are a tribe when they come,
In thrice tumbling all over the place,
Proving a point nonetheless,
Nothing to own and lose except love,
Which they had aplenty to give,
Guarding us and the family,
And he was the master though less.
Mongrel on the road left to die,
Sick pup without a home whining,
For care and a bigger thought,
Whence he had a home poorer,
For people with heart larger than world,
No one bothers what comes on the way,
Thoughtless they are whence they
See afar wonderful life has passed by,
He saw to carry him home to a new life,
Cared for, and living with him he knew,
He had reached the destination,
Some place he can call home,
Be part of a bigger clan which never
Existed for him to be alive long,
For the days are long and nights cold,
To be left alone on the street is,
Not any living being's right,
But they cleaned and bathed him,
Not just of the mud and the void,
Inside the heart of hearts,
He looks at the sky and whines,
Thanking HIM wherever HE is.

8
LIFE WITH MONGREL

Tis day again to wake up to,
The perceived beauty which is,
Finite to describe and feel,
Am I part of this which evolves,
And is changing in nature,
Every time to the beholder,
Still probing the depths whence,
He walks down to water my roots,
Where I am tethered to earth,
Secured watching the sky above,
Piercing the earth below with roots,
Deep down into the terrain,
The hardest earth and rock down under,
I grow boughs up above and feel alive,
Where I feel one with the mother,
Who gives birth to creatures all,
And takes them back into herself,
Whence she herself merges,
Into the Undefinable & Endless,
How much do we all expect him,
At this time to visit us with the
Nectar of life which will flow thro'
Our roots to reach the tender leaves,
He comes with the mongrel in tow,
Sniffing the air for new scents,
He is one of a class not a pup,
A tail that does not wag to wish,
Folded between his rear legs,
A mouthful of piteous whine,

Journey

Eyes and mouth drooling,
He looked a lot of mightful shame,
Trying to be one fuddled bundle,
And taking to him as his mom,
Who gave him what he missed,
For him he was the perfect pup.

9

NIGHT

It never was, It never is,
The dark wide open expanse above,
Which ends and is also endless,
Adorned with the diamonds,
Peeping out of their shells,
Ones with a swagger and staid,
The ones with a twinkle so nigh,
A bright moon lighting the carpet,
Studded with the tinsels,
Cotton balls in the foreground,
World silent except for the,
Occasional cries of cats in heat,
Splitting voice of the owls,
Whine of the mongrel shut out,
Beings of the night snooping,
Dried leaves rumpling under their feet,
Snaps and slithers of snakes,
And many more which are,
My neighbors silhouetted,
Rustling their leaves to,
The soft winds hailing me out,
Time to hang up and take a nap,
Everything goes silent for a time,
The dew settling on my pithy leaves,
The crowing cock heralds one more,
Of the too early morning,
Where dawn was near and night,
Fading away with the light,
The sudden pitch of the birds awake,
In the morning ends a night so dear.

10
Dawn

Everywhere the light pervades
Even within the tiniest cracks,
Worms squirming to announce,
The cacophony of birds chatting,
In multiple languages,
Salubrious dog stretching woof,
Squirrels chasing nothing,
Occasional snake basking,
Chicken clucking in a team,
The Mongoose chasing easy prey,
Early bird cooing his presence,
Life into the day which has arrived,
I wait for my lover who is near,
Who loves everyone not afar,
Watching from above too far,
Invisible to the eyes of flesh,
Presence I can feel all around,
Day and nights, long and short,
In low and the mighty and the least,
Its breath of the supreme,
Blowing away everything,
To leave an engulfing,
Sound of Silence heard,
To the Saints not here now,
Bubbling up again to create
The life which ceases to exist,
In him also I realize the universal
Love unrelenting, nurturing
With a caress, and an admiring look,
All troubles weaned away,

In an instant not too small,
He is there as ever to watch
Sprightly leaves waving away,
The boredom seldom known,
Of Life too small to measure,
In the infinite ocean of love,
In the days to come to merge,
To be One with the Supreme.

11
EARTH

The cradles of Love in her Bosom,
The crimson tides flowing,
Everywhere never ending,
Whipped up from the depths,
Nurturing her children far and wide,
Never awake and asleep even,
Not too much for her dear ones,
Full of life and strength and what not,
She cares and not cares for what,
Is nurtured on her laps,
Beckoning the sun and stars,
Days and ensuing nights darker,
To shower their radiance on beings,
Tiny and huge to be on her,
The bumps and curves of beauty,
Enchanting to behold shining,
To the meek and the mighty,
Bearing all equally without fail,
Knowing no Caste nor Creed,
Is it her silence or the scent,
Belching fire, breathing gases,
Its destruction when she heaves to
A mystery shrouded into,
Nothing when delved deep,
Whereupon this wide expanse,
Was I born to be nurtured,
With all creatures claiming,
Supremacy over the other,
When she creates, watches,
Over them in the sun, rain,

And the darkest of nights,
Helps them grow mighty and low,
Does she weep when they fall,
She still takes them to her,
Innards holding her children,
Near her heart to create more,
Creatures Unique.

12
WATER AND RAIN

That which is heaven sent,
That which has names in multitude,
Suspended below the Heavens,
Invisible in the making,
Assuming forms and colors,
As the environs beseech,
Flowing free uncontained,
Formed nowhere, disappearing
Elsewhere without any notice,
Feeding mighty rivers and streams,
Nature's softest arm to soothe,
And to smite the unknowing,
The life blood in my veins,
Pulsating thro' to the tiny,
Nerves on the toes of leaves,
Part of the day and night,
The clouds travelling so high,
A collection vast and dark,
The soft cotton balls soaked up,
Ready to explode in a torrent,
They arrive with the tantalizing light,
And the terrorizing booms,
Creatures searching for hideouts,
On the arrival of first drops,
Feel that patter very regular,
Coursing over my barks and leaves,
Drenching this happiness glorious,
Once in a while and not every day,
Streams of pearls painting a new
Picture on the face of the earth,

Exposing my roots time and again,
I claw desperately to the soil,
To stay but am swayed with the
Forces that are not in me but
Exterior to my senses and body,
I take birth again to view this
World which sustains me in ecstasy.

13
AIR AND WIND

It is a tiny touch, a pat, an embrace,
That is what he is everywhere,
Trailing through tiniest of the nooks,
Sweeping over plains, in forests,
Rustling leaves and shaking boughs,
In fury does not care for the mighty,
Tender as a toddler and warlord brazen,
Skipping from space to space,
Carrying clouds afar and near,
Tickling them to shed their rain,
Dumping shifting sands elsewhere,
What he cannot do either,
Ever present in light and darkness,
No human sees him except in action,
Lives exalting in his presence,
Where and when he will strike,
To play with whatever he wants,
Is left to Him to point to,
He is part of this wide world,
Most feared and loved dear,
He is in me, out of me everywhere
Where I might look and look,
Nowhere to be seen else,
Air, breeze, wind and storm are one,
Names too many to comprehend,
The source which was one and will be,
To be felt only when he grazes through,
He makes me and breaks me also,
To provide and hinder life,
Never in world confined to spaces forever.

14
THE SPACE

Too much of an expanse to match,
On the earth too small suspended,
Thither by invisible forces bound,
By orders of The Supreme,
The luminous one swims along
In day to complete his task,
Undeterred by whats below,
In that bright expanse lighting up
The low plains and rocky mountains,
Path undetermined never known,
Whence the stars and luminous planets,
Too many moving along,
Ones with legs creeping past,
Tails trailing long and shiny,
Where I am rooted do I see,
The shiny clumps spread far and wide,
No beginning and no end but
For the horizon must be the limit,
To decide is the one who sees,
Beyond the stars and what,
Small they seem in a twinkle,
A falsehood so far away,
Burning away with the time,
Lovely and lasting for the night,
The bright wide canvas holding them,
Immeasurable stretching too deep,
Changing constantly in variety,
Matching what's inside me,
Limited is the vision which never
Seeks the depths which was the same.

15

THE MENDICANTS

Breeze gentle as a toddler turns a storm,
Whipping dust and dried leaves,
High, dancing to the tunes of the invisible,
Boughs mighty gyrating crazy,
Leaves torn from their lofty perch,
Am I stretching too far to hear,
The roar of a broken branch,
Somebody bleeding bare,
Pain wafting through the grime,
Mad dance coming to an end,
And he comes with the pain shared,
Magic in his hands to cure,
Handful of earth and a tourniquet,
Secured and soaked to mend,
Blood and tendons bare steeped in love,
And a healthy day not far away,
The touch that transfers love,
How we yearn for that in days,
Of distress so deeply felt,
When wounded deep and bleeding,
Whence there is thirst hunger,
Then he humbly feeds us with the
Gruel so slimy and tasty,
Love written all over his face,
Do we hear the hum of a prayer,
Soothing the distressed and broken,
Soulful hug promising company,
Maybe forever that's what I feel.

16
Seasons

Evident is the change in my state,
With changes in the elements which,
Control and feed us, being with us,
Nurturing, tagging and guiding us,
Where they become violent,
In that mad dance where
We suffer that day in silence,
Tis the overabundant nature,
Eating away our lives in the present,
Whence the mongrel stopped,
Talking to beetles and up our stems,
Food and water in abundance,
For him it was an aversion,
Mouth tightly shut without any noise,
Making valiant efforts to scare,
To no avail he is failing,
With a sordid face does he make
The trip to the mendicant for a cure,
With his master so caring,
Cured and hearty does he speak,
With his tricks so cute,
Oh, does he grow to be big enough,
Wishes can be huge and truth small,
That fits in everywhere for us.
Even where humans don't exist
In flesh and blood.

17

MY LOVER

Where's life inside me,
Is it in the innumerable veins,
Taking the fluid from below,
To exhale in the expanse above,
In the bark, leaves, roots,
He feels life and love in me,
In each and every part,
Visible above the earth,
All over, I come to life in,
His soft scent in the air,
Gentle caress of the leaves,
Of wet mud oozing through
His fingers on my roots,
Of the inquiring gaze at,
The breezy touch which plucks,
Leaves grown old with time,
The tender checks of my stem,
The loving hugs of my physique,
And the all knowing admiration,
That flows out from his hands,
To drench me in droplets
I love him all over,
What is there to hate,
In this world where I am,
Beauty has to be perceived,
Love felt deep inside,
In the veins and blood,
I Feel him everywhere,
In me, in my life.

18
MY LIFE

Is it that our roots hold the earth,
Together that it is always moist,
Cuddling together to stay,
Sources which are inside
Water is always nigh to everyone,
Where is it closeted,
Is it the water that leaves us,
Makes our body moist,
Is it our beckoning that brings,
Down the rain from above,
Is it the elements that bade,
The skies to rain down,
It is always a regular cycle,
Directed by the elements,
Diverse in many forms,
Thirst driven by the Sun,
Sucking the water deep,
From the earth,
Through our veins,
Am returning what I took,
From earth to the air,
What goes in has to leave,
The shell without notice,
Am only a guide leading,
With the path laid out,
To conduct the vital energy,
But on top and below,
Life on earth nourishes life,
Even on the barren sands.

19
BLOSSOMS

The season inspiring a change,
The change ordained by nature,
Not stopped by any other force,
The shoots lithe and sprightly,
Waving away to the breeze gentle,
Satiated neighbors in this grove,
There are quite a lot,
Happiness aplenty within,
And outside radiating with,
Blooming blossoms blanketing
The leaves and bough,
Scent in breeze of blossoms so many,
Wherefore he is proud to behold,
Humans never were happy,
With things simple, but him,
So many blossoms in his garden,
Waiting to be collected,
To be offered to the Supreme,
Varied in color and scent,
Enticing for the old and young,
But not for him who does,
Not maul the blossoms hard,
Leaving some on the branches,
For the admirers to drool at,
The ladybugs arrive in a swarm,
Feeding on the flowers,
It is a feast for them in multitude,
They look beautiful, not on me,
It is pain everywhere,

They are content munching,
In their favorite feeding grounds,
He is trying to fend them off,
They keep coming back.

20
DEJECTION

The seasons wonderful,
Pretty enough to boast about,
Merry enough to dance,
To the tunes of nature,
Whence humans miss,
In their own world,
An Emotional warp,
Thy name, humans,
Cloaked in flesh and blood,
I see him cradling wrinkles,
In a face drawn out,
There are no chimes Sweet
Anymore in the air,
Withering happiness,
Spreading like a plague,
The blossoms and the lush
Garden is not the end,
No consolation from beings,
The mongrel slinks with,
His head to the ground,
Moments to hours and
Laboured breath,
Silence becomes the norm,
He is not himself,
Suffering untold,
Within himself,
And one day he left us,
For days to come.

21
MELANCHOLY

He is not present now,
Nor did he leave in a huff,
Nor did I do anything wrong,
Nor did I waste away,
Nor did I cheat and annoy,
Nor did I wait for him,
Nor did I throw tantrums,
Nor did,
I expect him every morning,
To cuddle me close,
Neither do I cry,
Neither do I whine,
Am not human to feel,
Am insentient too,
That's what the designation is,
By whom no one knows,
Behold, every being born,
Are with the karmic force in them,
Helping them, till they depart,
Lo, I seek him where I could,
Worthless this search,
For what do I search,
A love lost nowhere,
Without existence,
With no beginning,
And no ends also,
Affecting me all over.

22
WOOD CUTTERS

The mist and the fragrance,
Heavy in the air till he arrives,
Cannot see what is there,
His rays creating rainbows,
The early morning dew chills,
The leaves and the stem,
The weather has changed for good,
The chirping of birds more happier,
Where is happiness in me,
The wood cutters arrive,
There is the survey all over,
Gooseberry overgrew the limits,
Who decided that today,
The limits for our growth,
The advisers overjealous,
There is pain in the air,
The branches cut down,
Pleas for mercy swoop down,
Humans never had the ears,
To listen to our screams,
The scythes are sharpened,
It is very simple to cut down,
The roots cut out of earth,
The spirit slow in departure,
Mass of leaves, boughs and roots,
Strangled to an ultimate end,
Homegrown to be destroyed,
Indeed, life is short for humans,
We are witness to the generations.

23

DEATH

And he died one night,
The mongrel running feisty,
Performing feats dainty,
To behold lovely,
Too young to go,
But not too late to love,
Whence sickness overtook,
Affecting his throat,
Hoarse with the pain,
Averse to food and water,
In those final days,
Awaiting the master,
Stoic and steady,
Who was faraway,
With a wish to bid
Him a farewell,
Whither he lay struggling,
His apprehensions,
Fear unanswered,
Scratching the door,
For one mad dash,
For the escape which never was,
His friends crying in unison,
Watching the spectacle,
The legs flailing,
Tongue lolling in and out,
The spasm of the body,

Breath being drawn out,
And he left for an abode,
Best suited for him,
Was it love in cruelty.

24
FAREWELL

Death can be slow and painful,
Not for the brave,
Who are very much aware,
It comes after the long wait,
First on the visible earth,
Buds shriveled, burnt in the heat,
The tender leaves dry away,
Growth extinguished,
The leaves dropping away,
Daily food denied,
The green stems disappear,
The barks fading into tinder,
The stem wrought into a twig,
Devoid of the essentials,
Drying up with the day,
The sap evaporating slowly,
The dewy nights and morning,
Do not inspire a life in the wood,
Gathering dust in every pores,
The roots wait to waste away,
He walks in unbeknownst,
With the sceptre to direct,
Me to abandon this shell,
My wish to hold on wanes,
My Departure is nigh,
Hopes turn to dreams,
Within and without,
They are happy in the union.

25
REUNION

Humans, what is the search for,
What are the motions for,
When you have everything now,
Need is to live,
Need to indulge is greed,
Why you forsake the roots that,
Fed your hunger and thirst,
What is defined and what not,
All beings equal in the triad,
Whence the escape?
And he left from here,
Seeking what, leaving us,
Distraught pining for him,
Aren't we his loved ones,
Where do I search, where,
I seek in the air, in the warm sun
In everything I could,
To disappear on the way,
What do I seek,
Where' re the seeker and sought,
When both are in each other,
Where do I hold, when I am to hold,
Which do I leave, when I am the one,
Where do I seek, when to seek within,
The vast expanse I see is from within,
When there's nowhere to go,
It can be the anywhere inside,
It is dawn of many thousand suns,
And I am no one.

HOLLOW BLOCKS

It was a block which slipped,
On the foot below the safety lines
The mortar lining the shoes,
Toes crushed in the fall,
Inexorable pain remains,
Safety shoes do not hold,
Only fault is yours,
Decides the safety officer.

Medics dressing the wound,
It is a learning for them,
Huh, wounded by the block,
It will be weeks to heal,
What about work,
And the money earned,
Worries are for laborers,
Not for the executives.

An unpleasant ride back,
Bumpy, sweaty to the skin,
Waves of heat in the air,
Mirages on the lonely road,
Winding long to the temporal,
Overpowering nausea left over,
Tryst with painkillers to continue.

Unbecoming conditions on arrival
To a camp that is decrepit,
To rest for the nights only,
Days are with their add-ons,
Fraternal Issues unresolved,
The steady stream of visitors,
The many clucks and huhs,
No one understood how.

The leg supported on a stilt,
Plans for days to come,
Enormous in the vacuum,
Cash in short supply,
Healthy food a question mark,
Monetary arrears to be repaid,
The lender's hollow soothing,
Will give you one month.

Wife's futile sobs on phone,
Efforts to draw a brave face,
Children's innocent queries,
Momma's loving reassurance,
Dad's mindful entreaties,
Nothing in short supply,
To soothe the pain evoked,
Very deep inside.

Every move is a pain,
The foot cringing with heat,
The desolate shacks with
Eight crammed in on shelves,
Space never was a problem,
Men tumbling around merry,
Every night with the liquor
Consumed on the sly.

Come day and the noise,
Buses honking and rush to queue,
The habitual wish to rush out,
The search for the crutch,
The animated watch of the milling,
It's a stagger not steps,
On the crutches so new
Up and down the aisle.

The old man next door helps,
Where was he all these days
To train the single leg to trudge,
On a support not enough,
The all knowing smile,
The useless old man today,
Teaching the guy to walk,
The smallest creations ignored.

Too many things to unlearn,
It is a rare female giggling,
Man walks out with the girl in tow,
With a ruddy face he leaves,
Not to be included in the shorlist,
Of worries for the morrow,
It stuck somewhere, crash,
Mind boggling pain and
The missing floorboards.

Was loss of concentration,
Concerned hearts consoling,
Which doctor to where,
Expired insurance, no cash,
Treading on a razor's edge,
No passport, visa delayed,
Nowhere to go, pain,
It's all in the crazed mind.

Daily checks with camp boss,
Answers are not forthcoming,
Critical decisions to be taken,
Walloping the overworked brain,
Too many cooking the broth,
Putting in their efforts,
Tis the advice which doesn't cost,
Results left to cool.

The office cool and neat,
Secretary in outfit from space,
The repetitive video on the TV,
Continuous enquiring looks
Vanishing executives in suit,
Occasional entreaties to wait,
The wait long enough to bore
No one to answer the needs.

The day is drawing to a close,
People ready to leave packing,
Someone recalls a person dancing,
In the corridor on a crutch,
HR walks in suave with the charm
But it was your fault,
Company would have penalised,
But for the efforts of think who.

The sermon long and devious,
The end not in sight,
Saab, do I get medical assistance,
I do not have Visa, nor insurance,
Oh, it starts again and continues,
You did not understand,
A passerby helps in simplifying,
So clear nothing more to clarify.

No more questions to ask,
Passport with company, visa?
Further down which blanks to fill,
No more except the tears of despair,
What next and wrong answer,
Come tomorrow to discuss,
Oh, missed the fact of crutch,
I will call you to finalise.

Human resources department,
People achieving what,
Have better salaries and perks,
Did they get my visa,
Never had a department,
For my herd of livestock,
Was enough to feed them,
Take care of each one in turn.

The trudge back to the edge,
Who will give a ride back,
To the safe environs of camp,
Search and calls begin,
Locating a helpful driver,
The looks quizzing on the leg,
No space in the pickup,
Happy to stretch in the rear.

Camp boss has become edgy,
Authority circumvented,
He is sulking with vengeance,
Left out for the annual mela,
With some crocodile tears,
And people dancing drunk,
Oblivious of the morrow's,
That is the punishment meted.

The melancholic air deepening,
No news is bad news,
Old man takes by hand,
To his mighty small creation,
A kitchen garden in the open,
Of hollow blocks fencing,
Earth transferred from fields,
Afar in the desert.

The basil leaves dancing in the wind,
Free spirits awaiting no one,
Hearty and entertaining,
The leaves covered in dust,
Exuding freshness all around,
The mango tree on the front,
Kids playing in the shade,
Yearning inside never subsides.

Days grow into weeks,
Developing pain unbearable,
Temperature running high,
Spasms and delirium sets in,
The mind weaving webs,
Wife waving goodbye,
Angels holding hands crying,
Was that in the airport!

Nostril itches with the odor,
Nurses moving around,
At last in a hospital of sorts,
Sanguine atmosphere,
White everywhere and clean,
The nurse is very comforting,
But leg is very numb,
Devoid of any feeling.

Two days now and free,
Moved next door and normal,
Sense of missing something,
Queries reveal the missing,
You lucky bloke you did not die,
But the toes had to go,
Your sponsors did great,
They brought you here.

JOURNEY

Not to miss something,
Which was granted by Him,
Now there are no earnings,
Except what was lost,
Fitted without spares,
Its short the lost feeling,
Can see people in headdress,
Thrusting a paper in hand.

Instruction given out,
Does not reach the destination,
Something stuck in throat,
Stomach starts churning,
The tears flowing non-stop,
Figures on the cheque,
Barely legible except,
The zeroes that stare.

Returned in a stretcher,
The concerted looks of pity,
Transforming to happiness,
Smile on creased faces,
Like the beautiful sunrise,
Tis a welcome of sorts,
For someone saved,
From the jaws of death.

The hum of the air conditioner,
The wall clock ticking out,
The dimly lit room with rays,
Peeping in through the glass,
Pasted with actors' facia,
There is the shelf above,
Puckered with signs of bugs,
It is the frightening boredom.

The regular dawn and the noise,
The loss is now registered,
Who did what and why?
It is unwritten and unclaimed,
No more to loose here,
Money does not make it,
Maybe the knowing smile,
On the old man's face,

Huh, son glad you are back,
Now what will you do?
No simple answers,
I will see you every day,
You have not lost everything,
Still you are well and alive,
I will walk with you,
Till you are cured.

The old man has his friends,
The one eyed cat, a lame dog,
He talks, walks and lives,
With these in his shack,
And some plants rare,
He looks a typical bedouin,
Accents and the wild looks,
Maybe not in the heart of hearts.

The old man brings food,
Wonder how so tasty?,
But the scare was real,
An old man without identity,
Not signifying anything human,
A vagrant who walks anywhere,
Wastrel who does anything,
Does not do any work also.

It is the curiosity which moves legs,
The shack with tin roof,
The dog marking his territory,
The window reveals him inside,
Merry and singing aloud,
Bare hand serving as the ladle,
The aroma of food overpowering,
The dog and cat dozing happy.

That was creepy and scaring,
Sleepless night follows,
Old man at the doorstep,
Those soft and deep eyes,
That churns out the heart inside,
The morning rays behind his head,
Forming a halo unearthly,
I did not see you last night.

What to reply and what not,
He does not care for,
The dog limps in untidy,
Cat meows in the distance,
They are perfectly at peace,
It descends very slow,
That peace of mind,
The whole world moves away.

It is enthralling like a dip,
In the ocean open to skies,
Riding the waves happy,
Is it fear that holds back,
To explore the depths,
What it might hold,
Difficult to come out,
He has cut it short.

He has walked out,
Snap and the land appears,
Where is all this leading,
The strange feelings,
The leg, feet and the pain,
The mind going still,
No realization of anything,
I have become a lunatic.

Old man has returned,
Doubts arising in multiples,
You love to query, but,
Know you are the answer too,
Chacha says, smile in his face,
Identity lost somewhere,
Family too far away and near,
Life is happy without need defined.

Days trudge into weeks,
Drudgery is not the word now,
The life is turning more lively,
The pages turned are lighter,
The loot is off the head,
Unloaded where it can be perused,
The mind is wiped clean,
Where there was too much.

Not a day passes by without
The presence of the fakir,
Talks, laughs and mimes,
The eclectic clarity he had,
In all belied the appearance,
The sense of shame is gone,
Wherefrom and what I am,
Has disappeared in his presence.

The long restrained breaks out,
What faith does he belong?
Divinity is love and
Love is the faith and life,
Which feeds the whole world,
Love never denies anything,
It is in you, me and everywhere,
Love makes you immortal.

Humans do not have faith,
Are insecure without faith,
Insecurity is fear and hatred,
Hatred spreads death,
And countless vices and sin,
Now there is confusion,
And mayhem everywhere,
Who hates who, no one knows.

Humans who kill for pleasure,
Humans who kill for cause inept,
Who do not abide by laws of nature,
They exist in this world and more,
Saints who will save them,
Will come but in a while.
Humans who hurt people with tongue,
They are the vain and pompous.

Compassion never comes with birth,
Nobility is bred by character,
There are no more human saints,
Who walk the earth like ancients,
Everyone now traces the character,
To another living being on earth,
The noble cats of the forest,
Or the animals feasting on carrion.

The high flying kites and vultures,
As also the hares and rats,
The peacock and the parrots,
Snakes and the pythons,
Scorpions and centipedes,
Fishes and the sharks,
Every being relates to humans,
In their character distinguished.

Notice the cat in play,
Catch and let go and wait,
Play dead and you are safe,
Moving quarry feels the claws,
Cats love to play till death,
Dead meat is not for feast,
Humans play cat with the weak,
Seeeking pleasure in their pain.

These are the human beings,
Who trot as the gentile in world,
Surrounded by minions vain,
Seeking them as their lord,
Feeding off their discourses,
Their heart filled with hatred,
Concealed under a genial cloak,
Do they choose their victim.

With care akin to mouse in the trap,
Tormenting their victims with words,
And actions base, loathsome,
Driving them to sin and death,
There are more vermin to know,
Preying on other's efforts and industry,
Never do they extend a hand in need,
The immense joy is to create suffering.

You have encountered these on the way,
On the way to release from here,
A prison never worth the deal,
And dreams of the near and dear,
Wise counsel does not help,
These humans who do not mend,
Wherefore, learn to keep away,
As these are victims of their own folly.

Hare in the forest has to survive,
With hyenas and the lion and tigers,
Remember the kite has to alight,
To rest for a peaceful night,
The kings also merge in dust,
Saints also reach this earth,
The wonders and structures,
Will be part of a dusty history.

Still it is very much disturbed,
Old man has dropped a stone,
To make the waters muddy,
Wherefrom he gets these,
Trail of ideas convoluted,
This is making the mind turn,
Into circles and a whirl,
Only to stop at a naught.

Plaster is gone now,
Counting the missing toes,
The feeling to stretch the toes,
The abrupt end to the signal,
And the disappointment,
Old man has a chuckle,
What did you lose, son,
You have not lost anything.

You do not lose, what is not yours,
What you are is a mixture,
Of various elements,
That will decay one day,
You try to possess,
What is not yours today,
Tomorrow and ever,
Till it merges in the elements.

Misfortune never chose the ones,
Time marches on ever changing,
What you are today is not true,
For the morrow which might be,
Pain and happiness are short,
Today's pleasures are pain next,
Choose your pursuits wisely,
You never were what you are.

Humans are hollow blocks,
The block is closed on five sides,
And open on one side,
Soft earth heaped in the hollow,
Can grow trees mighty,
That will survive for eternity,
Humans are closed on all sides,
But are hollow on the inside.

Do not be steeped in a gloom,
Step out and speak for what is right,
Victory and defeat are only relative,
It is your mind which seeks them.
You do not deserve any punishment,
Taunts of humans with cats mind,
Does not deserve any action,
He was right in all respects.

It has stopped, the flood,
Of thoughts so pristine,
A fresh shower in the falls,
Carrying essence of herbs,
The mirror fraught with dust,
Cleaned in one big sweep,
The hatred that was lining up,
Has vanished like dew in sun.

The visit again was very short,
HR again in the big bully mode,
The straight talk had effect,
The tempo raises to a high pitch,
It drops to very cordial level,
The sponsor would discuss to close.
The visit to the sponsor,
Closes everything and straight.

It is a free world with no stops,
The day is sunny and the heat,
It is a dance everywhere,
Everyone on the road is happy,
Resplendent with the radiation,
The milling crowd is no more,
Alone and reaching the skies,
It is a feeling unmatched.

The freedom came with a freebie,
Unemployed is the word,
With the passport and ticket,
Ready to fly out albeit some toes,
It is shopping list that fills the void,
The list is long but cut short by orders,
Your arrival is more than enough,
But still the small wish remains.

To do and achieve list was long,
It is now very light and easy,
Not a heavy burden that weighs,
A ton on the shoulders,
Good enough to last for the life,
The metro and the lit up station,
The crowd oozing out of the train,
Wonder, all of them with loads.

A smile and shake of the head,
Still elicits turned heads,
Disbelief, pity and scorn,
Thrown without any price,
Am I ok or turned mad,
Still in senses all five of them,
It is a short journey which ends,
With still more pitiful looks.

More of the crowd in the mall,
People walking around things,
Inspecting, testing and tasting dishes,
Well dressed inside counters,
Everything for material comfort,
Crafted from nature by humans here,
Enticing people away from nature,
Helping cull the same once untainted.

It was a futile search for the old man,
Vanished in thin air, elusive,
So were his pets, gone,
But the belongings intact,
In the shack neatly arranged,
No one has seen him leaving,
People who saw him regular,
Elusive and disappeared.

Time to go and still waiting,
For that spark which set the fire,
The fire that is now brighter,
To light the way forward,
The heart aches to leave him,
The simple duty to say thanks,
And a good bye forever,
Would have doused the pain.

It is a journey filled with happiness,
And mounting misgivings,
Debts to be cleared and also,
The near and dear ones eager,
The daily expenses which are,
There is no end and no beginning,
A door closed and no door open,
For a walk through to happiness.

The family happy and jubilant,
The inquiries and checks,
On what is missing and lost,
The sweet smile of the children,
Slowly melting into the vagaries,
Which have to be met daily,
The rustle of the leaves,
Sounds very much foreign.

It is a new day to wish and plan,
The eager look on dad's face,
Turning to a question mark,
The announcement very heavy,
The plans still not very clear,
A little shake of the head,
You have to think carefully,
My son for the path is very hard.

There is the echo in the air,
What you have to wait for,
The Savior and the Messiah,
Are in you, the strength is in you,
Words of Saints are in books,
It is your duty to commit,
Work to the success and glory,
Chacha's words in the air.

There is the path never explored,
It's the mind which plays,
The hardest path is to success,
The easiest may please,
But never bring lasting peace,
Humans take the easiest route,
Success is but a single peak,
That is but a temporary stay.

There are no lot of answers,
Dad's concerns are many,
The answer's one and the last,
The green on the patch of land,
Overgrown with the weed,
Earth shoveled brings live worms,
She is alive and breathing,
She can sustain anything alive.

The wet soil curling around the feet,
The water turns up the finest,
Each and every grain unique in feel,
The coarser and bigger chunks,
Breaking up to reveal more secrets,
Mud flowing through fingers as silk,
The realization was never late,
To be alive on the destined.

She might not announce in ears,
She lives through the beings nurtured,
On her loving bosom fed with,
Lifeblood of the rivers coursing,
On her defining new ways and trails,
Unbeknown to humans the source,
And where they merge in the sea,
She is a mystery unto herself.

Destiny and fate are her tools,
Never understood by humans,
Blessings have to be bestowed,
Mother has to leave her grief,
To set her eyes on the righteous,
The seeds sown with the hope,
And the designs for the morrow,
Mere bragging rights claimed by humans,

The scars of years of negligence,
Doused on her and the results,
Many experiments for rewards,
She has borne with patience,
Now expressing her happiness,
The big heart that she has,
Visible on every minuscule grain,
Ready to serve her children.

Life is the set of hollow blocks,
Of dreams stacked to make a wall,
One more concoction cooked in her,
The elements trapped inside,
Seeking union with their source,
They crumble to earth and dust,
The cycle completes and returns for
Experts defining life times.

The celebration at the source,
Of living beings all on earth,
Knowledge that she is the very first,
To give birth to the beings on her,
The varied races and kinds,
Which appear and disappear,
The whole world unknowingly
Exalts in her discrete presence.

The piles and mounds of the earth,
Inspiring outpouring of philosophy,
There still are the futile queries,
Is it the future livelihood,
Does it pay your needs,
Who cares when you are not,
These are not the duties which bind,
Pay money which serves the family.

The earth which has sustained,
Beings varied on her for long,
Poor and dependant on her,
Families still on the necessity,
Toiling on her can still survive,
She has been the most kindest,
Showering her blessings on all the
Low and high, small and larger beings.

Realization even if late is divine,
What is defined as late and delayed,
For someone who has been there,
Ever watching over the families,
Of generations over and again,
The happiness is profound,
Living with treasure undiscovered,

Forgotten in vain pursuits.
She is smiling again after longtime,
Can feel it in the scent in the air,
Is this what they call Heaven.

REFUGEE

Wither forefathers stood on the land proud,
Built magnificent structures reaching the sky,
Fought wars terrible to save the land,
Were buried to merge in sand,
Heroes aplenty in the legends of the land,
Civilizations long cherished now erased.
There births and deaths were witnessed,
The relations multiplied far and wide.

People numerous varied seekers and sought,
City growing with the months and years,
Demand confirmed and trade flourishing,
Vendors sold their goods for immense profits,
Businessmen unscrupulous, but still,
Everything was affordable in aplenty,
Children partaking the joy and pleasure,
With education their parents were proud.

Elderly spent their time in peace,
Respect and love wafting in the air,
Places of worship wide open for everyone,
Ceremonies conducted with pomp,
Priests preaching Godliness on deaf ears,
Faction and faith governing love and hatred,
Travelers of world taking shelter for the night,
There was a brighter tomorrow to think about.

A sweet home to come back to after travails,
Of a mundane day punctuated with stress,
Business districts with their line of offices,
Vendors with their products lining the markets,
The mix and mash of tradition and the modern,
The plush cars and the traffic on the main,
The street hawkers unending vocal rhythm,
All blended a city which was once.

Calls of the birds and animals sweet in the air,
Trees that were the witness to generations,
The pools and water bodies with source anon,
Streams and gardens jewels on the landscape,
The orchards and waterlogged fields,
Gardens that were built by the ancestors,
Blending their fragrance with the air,
In the eerie silence of scintillating nights.

Multi story buildings and the hutments,
Posh gardens and the contrasting slums,
Sparkling rivulets and the garbage dumps,
Mega dams and the drought hit deserts,
People strutting healthy and the sick,
There was no dearth of God's grace,
The people happy and miserable,
Populating the land far and wide.

The proud nationals who walked the streets,
Anti nationals who fought for rights anon,
Politicians who promised everything,
Common man who is not moved to,
Think about the next day, month nor year,
Soldiers who labored for their payday,
Guarding the daily dynamic borders,
With neighbors who are friendly foes.

The magnificent picture which was,
Whipping up dust into the clouds,
The scent of the soil merging in the blood,
Structures of the ancient evoking pride,
Symbols of a deluded nation rich in heritage,
A land with boundaries with people varied,
Everyone had emblazoned in their hearts,
In letters of gold, the name motherland.

No more, spurned, driven away like cattle,
People migrating in masses too huge,
Themselves as the luggage they carry,
Some walking, some trailing, trudging
Some hitching a ride with someone,
Families once rich and poor together now,
Lots walking down the beaten path to,
A future unknown and uncertain.

They are fighting and killing people,
No one knows whom they are fighting,
Principles laid out in the drifting clouds,
The modern killing machines with a heart,
There is always an opposition to slaugter,
It is the human cattle which strays,
Animals were more noble to kill,
Only when there was the need.

The wave after wave of people,
Vagabonds in the multitude,
Society in shambles, there is no country,
Village or town either, no sense of belonging,
Identities lost, names meaningless,
Everyone has the same identity now,
Which everyone utters in hushed tones,
Tomorrow might be a better day.

The directions thrown wide open,
Beckoning with loving open arms,
No streets and no highways to tread
To anywhere which might be worth,
The plains and hills are one and the same,
The paths are different to the goal,
Which still by definition is freedom,
Which has lost its meaning now.

Once happy faces, creased with dust,
Toddlers walking longer than ever,
Older folk do not complain anymore,
Resignation writ large on their faces,
Carrying only what was decreed by HIM,
The land never complains about invasion,
The loving sands can take in everyone,
Whoever felt dropped on the way.

It is a hike for days together,
On earth cracked dry with the summer,
Oppressive to dry the beings on earth,
Feel the earth and air do not need the lot,
The same which fed and nourished,
Beings on earth and still kind to animals,
Still plenty on the offering for all alive,
Humans were the ones who never knew.

Mountains are not hurdles anymore,
Mighty rivers akin to streams,
The desert looks a sweet mirage,
The corpses without count on the way,
All are the dream of the blind,
Who looks back to possess anything,
This crowd has won over everything,
But the fear of an undefined war.

What was yesterday and tomorrow,
What was the summer and winter,
Who rules and who resigns,
The warriors or killers in disguise,
Who was friend and foe to be,
The neighbor or a sworn enemy,
All questions and talk of the past,
For the women gone silent now.

Once hunger was a need of the day,
Now hunger is a routine for the day,
Shedding weight was advised,
Now weight itself is awaited,
The count of family members,
Was the count of the whole clan,
Now, there are more fingers to count,
Who dropped where is marked on sands.

Death does inspire boredom now,
Graves have become shallow,
Killing has become nuanced,
Killers trained not to get bloody,
Traditions dropped by the wayside,
Traditional murderers are groomed,
Humans have evolved fast,
The tailed ancestors are elated.

The animals are free to roam anywhere,
The birds fly through every country,
Where was the identity, race, ethnicity,
Volcanoes blow without notice,
Earth conspires to tremble terribly,
Storms and deluge kill humans,
Mountains move themselves,
What faith do they belong.

Rivers and streams change course,
Deserts transformed to oasis,
Fertile lands turn bone dry,
Plains become habitations,
Cities and villages to forests,
Deserted monuments to temples,
Accepted as ways of the world,
But not the rightful livelihood.

What is there is of no value,
What is not there is a necessity,
Triviality kills, maims beings,
No enemy on the exterior,
The hatred is buried deep inside,
Bare necessities do not suffice,
No single definition for happiness,
Humans chase mirages so far.

Holiness and divinity are in robes only,
Heart and compassion are missing,
Words are being used to kill,
Believers, nonbeliever, Sacrilege
Who believes and who does not,
Belief was in eternal happiness and peace,
All bundled and swept away now,
For the lot which believes in death,

Aim is for short term pleasures,
Pleasure derived from suffering,
Inflicted on helpless, poor and women,
Wherefore they never complain,
Mortality is bliss for them,
The masses on a rampage to kill,
Instigated by the powerful,
Cattle in a mad stampede.

There is no distinction anymore,
Of innocence and the mature,
Maturity kills, innocence rejoices,
Parents inculcate the tradecraft,
Of killing and apathy to pain,
Love and work not for worship,
Love for sex and work to kill,
Are the slogans for the morrow.

Motherland and no more mothers,
A wide open slaughterhouse,
Carcasses strewn around,
Fit for consumption of hatred,
Where are the mothers teaching,
Their kids love and non-violence,
Everyone has gone hiding,
Protecting their little ones.

The stars in the night sky daily,
Myriad whoosh and the moons land,
Where and when is never known,
There is the exhilaration of watching,
And the apprehension of a hit,
Denial of being alive amid death,
Far from the days when death,
Was the occasion to mourn.

The days and nights are not legible,
The days are lit brighter by nature,
Nights are lit by the fireworks,
Of a war which has no end,
Cities and villages smoldering,
Nights are not cold anymore,
Now people are one with nature,
Beings with no possessions.

There are the camps holding many,
In shelters which are temporary,
The letters trumpeting the gifts,
Of people who are safe faraway,
The crowds spilling on to the path,
Every being pushing hard for rations,
For families and children hungry,
Which arrives once in a while.

The safest path is still not opened,
To escape from this place of hell,
What was once a Heaven on earth,
This migration to nowhere without,
Knowledge of what is ahead,
The migratory species now laugh,
At the beings migrating to nowhere,
At least they knew where would be.

The hillocks and the mountains,
Where we played and hid ourselves,
So sweet to look down on the plains,
That do not belong anymore,
Mirages everywhere, small and big,
Visible and invisible, everywhere,
HE is everywhere and has nowhere to go,
Is HE also a Refugee?

WOMAN

Salutations to the woman who is my mother,
Conceived and borne by her,
Months and the years after,
Playing multiple roles in ages,
A loving nurse for the baby,
Playmate and teacher of the child,
Moral adviser of the young boy,
Friend of the rebellious teen,
Strict matron for the youth,
Proud mother in law of wife,
Doting grandmother of the little ones,
Life's travails have left the mark,
Wonder she still is the same,
She never failed to deliver,
The love and affection in abundance.

Salutations to the woman who is my sister,
With the same mind as me,
Has held my hand all the way,
Partner in mischiefs perpetrated,
A solemn guide sharing the curious,
A teacher of lessons always mysterious,
One who likes smile on my face always,
The birds and animals explored together,
Went gazing and counted stars together,
The swing of the aruval and the trees,
The tantrums for the swing in the trees,
The honey combs and the myna birds,
Memories taking flight as birds,
Hanging around to protect me in trouble,
A sister who still guides me through trouble,

Salutations to the woman who is my wife,
The soul which has become essential part,
The wonderful nature's essential art,
Silent force behind the day's works,
That which accumulates she never shirks,
The latent talent toiling behind the scene,
Shaping the children's work day routine,
Infusing the spirit and morals in the mind,
Never refusing to be the best in kind,
Sharing the turmoils and the pain,
Etching best lessons not in vain,
An integral need for the society,
A woman high in virtue and piety,
Love bundled up into one wife,
To be together for a longer life.

Salutations to her, who is my daughter,
The source of unadulterated joy,
The curious and playful little toy,
Who gives nothing but love to one,
Nothing but my own flesh and bone,
The inspiration which drives the day,
Every other day should be a holiday,
To play and feel her pranks all over,
The future holds many more to savour,
Dreams many of the father for the one,
To achieve nothing less than the moon,
The worlds spin silent in your little smile,
Makes me lose everything by a mile.

Printed in the United States
by Baker & Taylor Publisher Services

Printed in the United States
By Bookmasters